# Mountain

# Breathing

# Mountain Breathing

Collected Poems
Volume 2

Richard Gartee

LAKE & EMERALD PUBLICATIONS

Published by Lake and Emerald Publications, LLC
www.lepublications.com

Library of Congress Control Number: 2013918811

Paperback ISBN: 978-0-9895104-4-8

Cover Photo: Richard A. Gartee
Used with permission.

Selected poems in this anthology were previously published in *Ann Arbor Review, Chris-Alice, Fifteen for Alaina, Two for Vilma, Black Cover Anthology,* and *Chrysalis.* Copyright 1970, 1974, 1975, 1976, 1977, 1979

*for Alaina, Kim, Vilma
and many more*

# Contents


Preface....................xi

The Poet....................1

Mountain Breathing....................2

Vista....................4

Like a Gardner Bends a Bonsai....................5

The Motion of the Poet....................6

Poems In Soft Paper Covers....................7

Last Lovers In Burgundy Province....................8

Lullaby....................10

Early Spring....................11

Myrtle Beach....................12

Pesach....................14

Near Miss....................15

Chrysalis Sister....................16

Prayer....................18

Praying....................19

Love....................20

Alaina's Birthday....................21

Fifteen....................22

Young Girls....................23

Instant Gratification....................24

What We Wants....................25

The Mind....................26

Four Lines for Ken....................27

Tides....................28

Unity....................29

Meeting at Myrtle Beach....................30

Rarity....................32

Women Shaped Like Wasps....................33

Glances at Dances....................34

She Likes to Dress It Up....................36

Mister Infinity....................37

Everyone Said....................38

Camp Town Races....................39

In Each Other's Way....................40

On a Warm Miami Night....................41

Grasses and Houses....................42

Dear Vilma....................44

Vilma Too....................45

Meeting Again....................46

Meanings....................48

My British Friend's Tea....................49

An Angel for the Government....................50

Learning Haiku....................51

Hopes Against Dreams....................52

Leave the Legends Alone....................53

Holy Water....................54

Balance....................55

Chanting.................................................................56

Shakti's Song.........................................................58

Dialogue from Earthside.........................................59

Kwan Yin..............................................................60

Not Two................................................................61

Cornucopia............................................................62

Offerings...............................................................64

Terrapin................................................................65

Flying Tree............................................................66

October 10th.........................................................67

In the Quiet of a Japanese Garden...........................68

Two Palms Whisper While the Sun Sets...................70

Coma....................................................................71

Two Veils..............................................................72

The Well...............................................................73

Art and Creation....................................................74

the material...........................................................75

Last Day at Convocation.........................................76

Departing..............................................................77

About the Author...................................................78

# Preface

Throughout the seventies and eighties Lake & Emerald published a number of chap books which are now out of print. Late in the decade an unfortunate fire destroyed all my personal copies as well as fifteen years of unpublished manuscripts. The blow to my creativity was such that I lost all initiative to write again. This is the story referenced in a poem in this collection, "Like a Gardner Bends a Bonsai." However, numerous friends came to my rescue, locating and providing me with their copies of my chap books. Literary magazines sent me back issues which contained my poems. Slowly I began to write again. Some of the new material was combined with versions of the chap book poems in a small volume titled *Black Cover Anthology*, now also out of print.

These were favorite poems of mine, no longer available to the public, never seen by newer readers. I decided to republish them in a new collection. As I began to assemble this collection I went back to the original chap books intending to incorporate them. I discovered some of the poems had been revised and incorporated into other books: *Chrysalis* and *Black Cover Anthology*. For poems that had multiple versions, I carefully compared all iterations and chose the version I thought best suited this anthology. For example, the poem "Shakti's Song" had several versions with different titles.

In addition to the material from chap books and *Black Cover Anthology*, I decided to add poems from whichever literary magazines I had copies. One of those poems, "Mountain Breathing," was originally published in *Ann Arbor Review*; it became the title piece for this collection.

I decided that the anthology *Mountain Breathing* should be more than a reprint of old poems. Several decades had elapsed between the publication of *Black Cover Anthology* and the development of this book. In the interval I had written several hundred new poems. So I included a number of unpublished poems written since the turn of the new millennium. The result is a collection that isn't entirely old or entirely new, but some of both.

In determining the sequence of the poems, I did not slavishly follow the order they had appeared in the chap books, but where there was a natural flow of poems in the original book I retained it when arranging these. However, many of the source books were written years apart. As a poet, I had experimented with different styles, rhythms, and voices at different times. I had also studied meditation and eastern philosophy over the decades that these poems span. I recognized that my view of the universe was reflected differently in poems from different time periods. Organizing poems that had similar ontology and/or narrative style together became an additional factor in my criteria. I also wasn't afraid to edit previously published poems, changing a word or a title or punctuation where it better suited my meaning.

The final result is a collection of poems spanning four decades that form a study in the evolution of a poet philosopher with feet made of sand, whose soul may sing OM, but whose eyes notice blond hairs on the back of tan thighs at the beach. Along the way are observations of how we think, feel, and interact with the people who appear in our lives and with the universe unseen. I hope you will enjoy the poems I have selected for this collection.

*—Richard Gartee, 2013*

# The Poet

Intensifying, illuminating
everyday events
the poet studies what others
have passed by
and brings them back
to that
which they have lost.

# Mountain Breathing

1.

    We follow a guide
along her exact path
step into each space
she has just left;
one foot to the other.

the song of each nostril
pulses with rarified air.
we reach at last, a mountain-top meadow.


2.

    Feet breathe rocks
of the path.
we follow light
scattered through our breasts
from an afternoon sun;

taste the chilled ozone
as we near the summit.


3.

    Moist field seems a
yellow-delicate green altar
honoring the process of
balance and the process of
law governing the turn
of an atom
or the evening of a planet.


4.

    Inhaling great waves of light
the Earth breathes twice
each year.

We have walked up to see the exhalation
begin.

Hearing the transition
take place, in
no more than a breath of seasons.


5.

Eyes close,
waiting in stillness.

We transcend even our own noisy
self
for this second,
within
as the current of life to death changes.

We stay
watching the hesitation
of breath thought
on a September mountain
when the aspens are gold
and yellow Summer tips
the scale to Fall
Sun hides golden rays
behind taller trees
Sapphire sky turns surprisingly cold


6.

Tentative, wary, observers reluctantly rise
to descend
weightless from balance

No one shall
be on this altar mountain to see in
the breathless death,
of Winter.

# Vista

Mountains and valleys of a life well lived,
make for a beautiful vista.
Though some were steep,
and some low, some perilous,
but some just took your breath away.

When seen from eight-one
they all seem to fit the perspective
and form a picture
of a life with its own beauty.

# Like a Gardner Bends a Bonsai

one year ago
the only poems left were those in magazines
or small books
and i felt finished with it.

but slowly a new work
came out and feelings changed
i found myself thinking
of new writings, collections, ideas

perhaps only the old works were separated from use
and a new being was forming
and i could watch it
with honesty and questions
detached study and hope

picking up my pen
i began forming these shapes
like a gardener
bends a bonsai
to his mind's eye.

# The Motion of the Poet

In each task the true poet
raises life to an art form
as naturally
as the breath
from the hill
moves the trees

When his poems
live within him
how can he do other
than express them
even in the motions
of his life.

# Poems In Soft Paper Covers

It started with poems in soft paper covers
typed on a manual typewriter
three hole punched
and bound with brass clasps

It began a fifty year gestation
stringing words into thoughts
like a tailor sews with threads
cutting and shaping the material
stitching the fragments into whole cloth
and storing them in cabinets and closets
seldom seen and hardly worn

And which of these stand the measure
of classic time
and which scream out of fashion?

If the tailor's eyes go weak
so the needle she can no longer thread
then it follows that when she
tries on those long ago garments
she must, needs, to stand
so close before the mirror
that her eyes are blind to any flaws

And if the silverfish have eaten
those papers
or the moths have eaten her cloths
does she see the naked flesh
pushing through the holes?

# Last Lovers In Burgundy Province

The village,
pastel from sunlight diffused
by a sheer veil
of cloud,

trees,
black stalks, barren, tall;
gentled, lent charisma,
by the contrast with
brown-russet bricks;

naked limbs over-watch aged
buildings four stories high.

White cloud light
brilliant on the windowpanes
glints from upper-story apartments
like afternoon shimmering off
an old man's spectacles.

Hot breath in a room,
second row from the top,
frosts windows.

While city eyes turn down
into their cups
last of all, two young lovers
make-out.

The damp chill of autumn
has bitten deep the others,
it holds them apart.

Alone they scurry
over winter fit streets
or crawl,
asleep, into their minds.

At sunrise the discards
of wine lie in spills on
the cafe floor
while three stories above
a last candle burns low;
in purple village shade
nothing seems left
but shadows of morning,
and lavender streets cooled too soon.

# Lullaby

Rapturous gods of nightfall
overwatch
as they lay braided to ecstasy
and cradled in bliss.
He writes a love song for her.

Soft earth
shimmering in bird notes
and tender morning pine
celebrates a pink daybreak.
She pays
this minstrel in coin
of soft breaths.

# Early Spring

The planet is warming
Spring is coming early

Buds are on the tulips
Boats are on the fjord

The fleet is anxious
for the sea
water rising
as the lovely girls are crying
good-bye

Northern ice is melting
As young boys are torn
Between the appeal
of warm down comforters
nestled against soft bosoms
or the bosons call in early morn.

# Myrtle Beach

sea oats stand like wobbly soldiers
around the dune line
the fiery gold orb in the sky pounds the
sand with photon after photon
scorching my back
while the wind sprays sand
over every object
and moves the heat
from place to place

the heat extracts every thought
and leaves me barren for what to write.
i had promised myself to set down a recent
remembrance of this journey
but have put it aside too many times today

i imagine it is cooler at
the water line
so i go there
to sit in a hot pool bath.
it feels like the salty whirlpool of a Jacuzzi
i once had in California

the sound of the waves and ocean
becomes dominant
they remind me somewhat of the
distant sound of traffic…
well perhaps sweeter.
i try to make the mind think of them as Om
but realize that if the ocean
and the traffic both sound like
Om

it doesn't really matter where i am

i pull on my shirt half-way
my shoulders are becoming redder
and will be painful if i don't;
my face seems to be achieving
a similar state but having nothing
to wear over it, i only turn away.

people keep passing by
picking up shells and placing them in plastic
bags
i keep feeling it is symbolic:
…old ocean,
the source of life
surrounding us, its presence and sound…
but they scurry around its edge gathering up trinkets
and taking them home in plastic bags

yet i am no better
trying to gather its flavor
or hot salty aroma
in twenty or thirty lines
while the sounds of God
pound on my ears
and sea oats stand like wobbly soldiers
around the dune line.

# Pesach

Alabaster skin and a bright green dress
Red hair and bright eyes
A young girl's smile
And a young girl's hand
in mine
And I have no idea of her age
or how to read her
but she feels nice
—is nice
like a searching soul
on the edge of something
she started seeking
and is sure to find

We eat and pray together
and talk together
and walk to her car

Miles later
away from there
that alabaster shines in my mind
and I have her then and there
just in my mind.

# Near Miss

Where went my
breath, my mind
when I noticed
your eyes
Your nipples showing
hard through your shirt
and I noticed them, too

Your waist was so slim
your attention so focused
but it was my heartbeat,
my breath…
I noticed them
dance with every
thought of you

And was I reading into it
or not?
I am so paranoid…
But you kept coming back,
kept talking to me

Are you thinking of me
as you drive away
the way I am thinking
of you?

# Chrysalis Sister

music played
a lithe poem in my head.
clouds spun from gold
glowed from inside out.

movements in light brown,
she trailed against grasses
so vibrant and green
they hurt your eyes.
the day we met.

moss-hung oaks
shaded her supple young leg
and stared, as did i.
she kicked at the weeds
and strolled by the beach.
her feet were made of
small sand
as were mine.

lost in music
played on sunday afternoon i
did not know the violin
crescendo became the lake
where the softest lady walked.
she reached out for the sun.

we walked out on our knees
chest deep in the water
but still on the dock
that sank when the lake rose.

the ladder
descended two fathoms
from the edge of the dock.
when we climbed down
and floated back up
we were walking in space.

we learned what one
gravity was not.
walking in space.

water cleared our eyes.
in a meditative state
we went down.
tanned arms tangled,
we merged and became
a point
which balanced the scale.
we were the fulcrum
of the atlantean lesson.

ancient wisdom.
recurred in our watery cocoon.
like toothless saber tiger relic
dredged from tar pit
to resurrection,
it no longer frightened.

in telepathic wedding
we learned of
chrysalis.
we stayed.
we did not breathe.

# Prayer

sometimes all love
about me
flows from you
and nothing is
above you
i see
your
face
in my mind
and know a faint
implication
of my own self.

# Praying

If you really hear
the small voice which
speaks your thoughts
inside your head
really speaking your deep,
deep prayers
you may be certain
they've been heard
for that You
           who hears,
that voice, pray,
does dwell in the same
heart space with
Saints of all your lives.

# Love

It is all so easy,
Love is;
only breathing,
opening,
being open.

What flows,
is what you allow to flow

Who lives in your heart
is who you keep there

I open
and embrace you
and you dwell herein.

# Alaina's Birthday

I raised my face to the window
where the wind pushed the rain in
and misted each cheek

cumulus clouds covered the sun
but illuminated the sky
with an alabaster aura

the stage lit
the leaves danced
on the ends of their branches like Sufis

the rain fell no harder than fog
yet the wild air stretched from the
earth sixty feet or more
beyond the top of the tallest old oak

and the moss swung
like mystic sisters
at play in the rain.

# Fifteen



Fifteen is delicate,
the fragrance of summer clouds
in the thunder.

# Young Girls

small ferns in the shade
near the door
swelter humidly
and dwell there
in relative cool
summer shadows

yet, like eyes grown heady
over mild flirtations
they go wild and spin
with the mind
thriving
like they'll never stop growing

tasting dew in the morning
and drying all day
learning
in the edge of summer darkness
movement and play.

# Instant Gratification

It was the night before her party
when she turned seventeen,
made me think about the urgency
everything seems
when you are on that cusp of life.
Made me think of a line I heard Carrie Fisher use.

When the Now,
living in the present,
isn't fast enough
finding the essence of your insides full of urges
to find more than you have yet,
to take it all in and be done with it

While adults about you rave on
about thinking in the future,
while philosophy classics command you
to think of the moment,

How do you do both without losing yourself?
That's something to puzzle later,
say after eighteen, because
for the moment, the moment is hanging here
like it's never going to end
And instant gratification, is just taking too long.

# What We Wants

What we wants
we gets,
and the trick's
in being careful
what's we want.

# The Mind

The mind
is a small
place to live.

# Four Lines for Ken

ego—death
like water is
strange &
guiltless.

# Tides

The mind is
like water,
ruled by the moon.

rising and falling
tidal waves
of thoughts
come and go.

some things seem easy
some difficult
just by the way they
are fastened to rising
and falling waves of thought.

# Unity

the only difference
   I can see
between you and me
is me.

# Meeting at Myrtle Beach

back at myrtle beach one year later
and of course, it's not the same.
a thousand billion
grains of sand have worked their way
across the shore

still, a hundred thousand
undressed homo-sapiens
walk and lay, brown and burn,
and talk and turn,
and try to turn each other on.

but i
am trying to be a different
i this year
to be smaller, less dominant
satyr seeking tan stimulations;
trying to pour less energy out the eyeballs
and more into the heart;

trying to sift a thousand billion
pebbles of light
from one set of cells to another
while you pass by me
smelling like cocoa butter
and hot eyes.

emotions take her to me
and suddenly we are lying on an
old tapestry
in the warm sun
her tan legs

like brown waters
glistening
with short blond hairs
thick and white
in the hot light

the mind wonders,
will i never weary
of watching
small blond hairs
on the back of tan thighs?
my vision seems to
bend toward the
creases of her bathing suit

she looks into my eyes
as we talk
i look into her mouth
or to her tanned legs
with their coat of small fur

it appear as if my
eyes
have directions
of their own.

# Rarity

it may be possible there is
no finer time to be alive
no better place in history to be than woman
young and free, just now

provided she be truly free
head uncluttered
rigid assumptions overcome
to play with joy and dance
with freedom and respect and love
and just enough struggle to provide
a slight pressure or tension
to uphold the illusion

like those ladies rarely glimpsed
now and then
one of a thousand
in towns of thousands.

# Women Shaped Like Wasps

He met a woman shaped like a wasp
and thought,
you know that's not natural
you know what that cost
       Counting calories
       dodging meals
       hoping it makes men
       want to cop a feel

When he tells her she's too thin
she says he doesn't know a thing
about what it takes to get work
in her world.
Then he feels like a jerk

He apologizes profusely
he tells her she's not fat
she pulls at her clothes
and thinks he's lying
to get her in bed

She's not wrong
he's dying to get her in bed
But not because she's built like a wasp
but because he's not yet dead
and only a dead man could resist
a move of her lips, a glance of her eyes.

# Glances at Dances

The two blond women dancing
with lesbian innuendo
The tall blond glances at me
measuring my reaction
alternately being engrossed in her partner
and checking if I am judging

Yet they were not for real lesbians
just testing their footing
in a fun night of flirting
with something that seems
adventurous and dangerous

Another couple, slow dancing
tightly embraced
her head on his shoulder
his eyes closed
softly gliding with the music
deep in the moment of holding her close
her eyes are open
and with furtive glances
alternately looking bored and
looking to escape her life with him

Yet when our eyes meet
she jerks her eyes away
as if I caught her
as if she thinks I read her mind.

The music changes
the dance floor floods
The two blonds return with a company of friends

and a tall black man who dances with style and grace
he dances with them all
And while they dance
one woman competes with him for her friend
and every once in a while her friend, the tall blond
glances at me across the crowed floor
Am I still looking?
Am I still noticing?
What, she wonders, am I thinking?

And he who is at the center
of all these glances
am myself glancing at the tables of seated couples
encircling the dance floor

He makes a move
And checks their approve
He sees them glance at him
and talk to each other
He imagines it is about him
Are they saying "he's pretty good"
or "look at that fool/thinks he's so cool?"

And all the while the partners
hardly ever catch each other's eye
When they look at all
they see the other's mouth
or feet, or hips, or chest
but never touch the other's eyes
with their glances.

# She Likes to Dress It Up

She doesn't emit
that much sexual attraction
but she has this polished look
that makes her attractive

She likes to dress it up in furs
and pointy toed high heels.
They seem to fit her pointy look;
like you would expect to see her
in those shoes even with jeans
—of course with jeans
she would roll up the cuffs
to show off her ankles
and of course the jeans
would be one or two sizes
too tight

The remnant of childhood braces
show in the habit of her smile
her lipstick always bright enough
to catch your eye

I think she likes to dress.
Give her an occasion and she'll whip
on a gown and matching high heels
and a personality
that she wears
like sparkly earrings.

# Mister Infinity

He put his bare feet on Florida sands
and thought rain clouds into non-existence
when gray storms threatened
our beach holidays.

When we first met
he carried two mirrors to demonstrate
that one mirror reflected into the other
created a multiplicity of images that reached
into infinity.
He called himself Mister Infinity
I named him a captain of infinity.
A woman made him a brass armband
of with the symbol of infinity.
He set it on a window sill in San Francisco and
its power burned down the house.

The kindest of men
he looks into their hearts and sees goodness there
and he reflects it in kind
but his mind like a knife,
cut through bullshit wherever he saw it.

He is truly one of the remarkable
men of life
who lives with his compassionate heart open,
my friend.

# Everyone Said

His mother said he was too pretty to be a boy

His father said his problem was
he grew up surrounded by women
who thought he could do no wrong

His wife said she loved the way he kissed

His girlfriends said
they didn't want him to have any other women

He looked up and said
I'm surrounded by vaginas

His friend said with envy, what a good life –
surrounded by vaginas.

But a Wiseman said his enlightenment
was just a pubic hair away.

# Camp Town Races

The first time he saw her
she was wearing a tee-shirt with
the logo, "Camp Town Races,"
it spanned her huge bosom.
They were introduced.
He said, "Do-da, do-da,"
And she laughed.

Later when they were alone
she pulled her shirt off,
a tattoo on her breast read:
"May the future me
change the whole world."
"It surely will," he said.

# In Each Other's Way

Like the moon and sun
light the day
and light the night
when they stay apart

but eclipse each other
when they get in each other's way.

# On a Warm Miami Night

## (Dialogue from Surfside)

The night, black,
the wind over white waves
washes the foam from their gray visions
The candle warms the room
with fragile light

      "Blow out the candle
      and I'll see you in the morning
      or turn out the lights and we'll begin,"
      he says.

let flow the fire
dancing and clinging
to the wick and tallow,
      he wishes.

Sputters
against the light of stars that flicker on
as the candle flickers out with a sudden wisp
of pungent smoke
rising from our good night flutters

it is out
but what subtle tension
the soul knows.

# Grasses and Houses

The silent drone
            of humming hands
        that fills the endless sea
                    of tears
            and sweat
covers the ears
                in deadly glaze
    of golden mists
        and raindrops
gone

the roaring thunder
                of the crushing waves
                as they smash against
                little grains of sand
                laying like a golden carpet
                beneath the foam
pounds against the ear drum

The heavy feet
            no one hears
trip clumsily
                over the neatly weaved branches
                that formed the small grass house
we slept in last summer

The umbrae shades
            pulled tightly down
            over the window of sunshine
        and the stars
                like tiny holes
                    in the black paper

flickered
        in unison
        with the lap,
                of the water
and I fell into your lap,
flickering in unison
                on the golden carpet

But now the white dry sand
                        scorched and yellow
                by the fire of the day

lies
        still warm
                beneath my bare toes
                and the grass house
                is a mangled bunch of weeds
under the black summer sky.

# Dear Vilma

I, dreamed of you last night,
dreamed of being, in Vermont
and seeing you there,
we talked and there was music.

It snowed thickly
in large lazy flakes
as we said, good-bye.

It seemed that I should write,
not because of the dream – really,
but because I just love you.

# Vilma Too

Before you're distant,
play for me, please
one of your sweet melodies,

Let me have
just a few notes for
my mind.
The mind, a worrisome thing,
which rattles around
in my brain
Give it a verse to which
it can beat time
when it dreams of your
sweet face
while you're distant from
the eyes.

# Meeting Again

Oh mother,
oh sister,
i have been you before.
exiting the journey,
the hot dusty road

when
in blistered speech the feet
call to be kneaded;
limbs are swollen and
your hands no longer reach

the cool ointment and bath of my
being, await your travels
completion.
O! where are your feet?

In a time, now generations past,
once, at the end of my path,
with the sweat of damp breasts,
you did oil and anoint
the feet that i wore

when bleeding, they
had been rubbed with the
granulated stone cut from time
and polished with the particles
of an ochre desert
you dried them with the silken
yarn of your black hair

This incarnation,

these hands, this soul, will
massage you with peace
oh mother,
oh sister,
where are your feet?

# Meanings

picking up apples
spilled on the floor
means:
meditation blanket unused
offering of fruit
pulled over by weight of disuse.

sleeping dog rolls over and growls
means: lazy body refuses to rise
means: no more staying awake late
no calls to California
no sleeping over mornings

three tones pierce desires
means: right woman not home
save your dime, listen
to intuition instead of dying
for a dial tone.
let sleeping dogs
be as they were.

# My British Friend's Tea

"A pot of tea in the morning
adds to a man
that brisk posh of things well begun"
he says to his kettle
as the day comes

he stirs his milk
and sweet
          to cup;
sniffs the steam
& sips the edge

his humor steeps
and becomes robust
as his foggy dreams
proceed to melt

by then the sun is
nine o'clock
and high enough
to dust the hedge tops
          with yellow light

He rinses water into
the china and sets his
cup in the sink
now he's fit to wear
his work-day leathers
and do whatever chores
can stand between
the proper-morning man
and his afternoon tea.

# An Angel for the Government

Today I met a man
who said he was an angel for the government
except his wings were on a jet plane for the USN
that burned a hundred thousand gallons
of kerosene in its lifetime
before he crashed a tree during a stunt dive in Texas

The tree grew on a hillside outside of Dallas
and the flies were buzzin'
around the pilot when they found him
six miles from the twisted site of metal
and blackened branches

Although his wings are smaller now
and dwell on a small closet shelf
he's still an angel in his story
and draws a pension from the Navy.

# Learning Haiku

New Year's eve, at twenty-one
I mastered the drunken art
of writing yellow haiku
on Central Park's moonlit snow.

# Hopes Against Dreams

We were fifty-eight
or near enough
when we gathered once again
We came to see,
I suppose, who still looked good
and who looked rough

Some women had obviously
endured the pain
that vanity required
and most of them were dyed
But the men were au natural,
bellies over belts,
and hair mostly gone

We were standing around
cold drinks in hand
when she heard he was single
She gave an involuntary squeal
that just escaped her mouth
like the sound of her heart
leaping against her throat,
forcing hopes against dreams
not quite forgotten.

# Leave the Legends Alone

Leave the legends alone
never go chasing the
peculiar characters you met
in your past
they are only archetypal appearances
in your history.

# Holy Water

The priest shakes his water
and they begin to be Christians

I don't know if this is the way
they really do it
but it couldn't hurt them
and it helps,
it lets us know who
has karma with whom

What else
could a man want from religion
than the chance to prevail
God's will?

# Balance

Some say it's all a question of balance
and some say it ain't no fun
but I myself say we all are one
How little it takes to change the balance
I am surprised it isn't more often done

Sometimes people are a constant source of
disappointment
with their shallowness of perception
and misunderstanding of how real and unreal it all is

A fast road and a soft curve
are all that some may ever need
but some need to have answers
that take you (by coincidence)
just where the road leads
and they drop what they have to,
to take it

Voyaging
back to the source
which lies in every direction
that I point my nose;
for it is from whence I came
always within

The source of the world,
in the gate of the soul,
there I take off my shoes.

# Chanting

The organ was playing
i began to hear singing

*Sri*
*Krishna,*

i breathed in temple air

*Govinda*

rich with golden chants.
they held my heart, like vessels.

my eyes turned upward

*Hari*
*Murari*

appeared before me,
with peacock feet crossed at the
ankles,
as blue as i had ever heard

*Hey Nartha*
*Narayana Vasudeva!*

the words
hung on the air like tones
on musical strings

the chants
the names of God.
went on and on through
cedar walls

i turned toward the side
stretched my legs,
so enraptured, relaxed, in love
with the sound of the songs

presence
there
again,

*Sri Krishna*
*Govinda*

this time standing beside
Christ
the two of them

*Hari*
*Murari*

communicating
something more esoteric
than i was prepared to
record
for my head was filled

*Hey Nartha*

and my heart with love

*Narayana Vasudeva.*

# Shakti's Song

In the dark hours
her energy kneels
in my door

Her vibes play
their song on my
spine
like she
could be Lionel Hampton.

# Dialogue from Earthside

"So,"
he said,
"I am everything in this universe
but none of those things I pretend
to be

"For I would worry myself
to be the flute
instead of the note played
or flute player

"I glow inside myself
like the very sun
and yet pretend to be only
a poor lantern maker."

# Kwan Yin

Her birth showed me
the incarnation of Kwan Yin
Chinese goddess who pours out life
onto the world

Then by her grace one night
I was sitting in a crowd
meditating
with my eyes closed
and seeing by her presence,
the form of Kwan Yin
in the world everywhere

And behind that vision
lay another
and in that, she, the Mother of the universe
The heavens compose
her body
twinkling with myriad stars
in her form
as she pours the force of consciousness
from her vase
onto the earth

On special nights
In her presence
bliss arose
and swept over
and melted me
with the waves
her fingertips
were issuing
as her many arms were waving
toward my heart.

# Not Two

Crayon picture world
on a carpet-thought wall
designed by smudgy fingers

Architect's smile covers his ears,
hiding him from the sand winkle,
who winks at the face in the
corner, where time flies,
and the guitar players, too.

All run from the man who is one
and not two.

All strive to pass
that paradox, and try
'til Charon waits scythe in hand.
And find he commands not the exit
but death,

For if you're two
and not one,
you're not one at all.

# Cornucopia

## Or the Killing of Kamadhenu

The cow's
leather fur
leggings,
her well heeled
hoofs
saunter green lawns,
graze, with brown
eye on early
morning awakening

Horses she heard
on the hard
road
halt
arrogant rider
brusquely dismounts

Tall emerald blades
brush the cavalier's
scabbard with dew

He skewers
the warm fat one

Herbivorous steak
tonight
will roast over
glow fired tree

Holy death
Ol' brown eye
will stroll
no more
on well-heeled feet.

# Offerings

The golden arches,
American's new altar
where they stop
to eat the fatted calf.

# Terrapin

Plodding assuredly across
the road
one pointedly
concentrating on
reaching the other side.

The threat of
vehicular juggernauts at
60 MPH
does not faze him.
Although his feet feel
the road tremor;
his eyes see not
the oncoming stranger,
far beyond his
point of view.

# Flying Tree

Just on Christmas Day the lightening
sliced a water oak
to the ground

Then it was in the middle of May
that I saw a flower shaped fungus
growing on the end of the log,
like an ivory daffodil

I bent to look more closely
and saw
the fungus which had eaten the fallen tree
was busily being nibbled
by some thin bodied flying insects

And the tree
(indirectly eaten)
lifted its cells on gossamer wings
to fly away.

# October 10th

The fog lifts lightly
as the crisp edge of a gray
morning
nibbles the ears.
Old time streets are
garnished in orange
and yellow memories
scattered like leaves
fallen over worn sidewalks.

Detach from a thousand brisk mornings
once crossed here,
and remember the embrace and shiver
earth mother leaves
just before she crawls
into quiescence.

# In the Quiet of a Japanese Garden

In the quiet of a Japanese garden,
distant from the city
and recessed from even the country road,
a master sat his disciple down
beneath the sweet smell of a large magnolia tree,
the largest blooming tree in the realm.
When its large, white, fragrant blossoms
first burst in spring
they spread open and fell quite quickly.

The first day he told the boy to meditate
until several hundred of the petals had fallen.
The boy could not count them,
having to look within instead,
so the master would count them
and let the boy know when he could leave.
Every day the number increased.

The blossoms rapidly flourished,
then were shed.
Soon they fell less frequently,
sometimes taking all morning
for their leisurely descent
to accumulate the assigned number
Gradually the master worked up to five hundred,
although fewer and fewer fell.

The tree, though thick with waxy green leaves,
was nearly bare of blooms
and merely full of seed pods.
The master said,

"Today we will half your number and add it onto the
whole."
So the boy began,
and when he had passed a hundred,
the blossoms softly spoke;
their gentle scent tingled in his nose.

For the first time
the boy was able to know how each petal fell,
to keep count, to know if this master
was accurate in his count,
He listened as each petal sighed.
He waxed in ecstasy.

When his seven hundred were completed he stopped.
The master feigned fury and shouted:
"What! You lout!
You can absorb yourself in hearing petals fall,
but cannot do simple arithmetic?
I said 'Take half and add it on to your number'
—you have another fifty yet to go!"

At this, fifty additional magnolia petals fell.

# Two Palms Whisper While the Sun Sets

Two palms stood
at the sun set,
one was thicker
than the other,
male and female.

Like lovers
in the wind, they spoke

    "Love
    is where the roots are."
said one.
    "So, Love is
    where you're planted?"

    "No," replied the other,
    "Love is where you plant it."

# Coma

Child of my sadhana
I saw you at death's door
and called to you
from where you slept
you opened your eyes
and knew what I said
as I told you I was thinking
of you always

And now I find I can't do anything else

I call out to you and ask you
what you see
when your eyes are closed
and you're so far away
You say dreams
and your eyes are light
like walking through a fog

I draw you back
and tell you to stay tonight.

# Two Veils

ONE

even as i held your thought
my heart was opened wide.
but as i stirred
becoming aware of
confusion inside
there pierced my gray
shadows
a ray of your love
a beaming perception
like intense golden
light filtered, dimmed
by self-deception.


TWO

words which mean
are not restricted to what they say.

hot wind carries more
than the cool breezes can blow
the weight of their presence
greater than their
sensual massage

what fool cons the stranger
and steals not what's given
freely
to any heart
open to reception.

# The Well

I am a well
you are an artist
I wait you to draw me
The water I hold
is yours for the thirst
if you drink it

If you only draw pictures
you take home only charcoal
if you sip of these springs
the water becomes you

But I cannot be other than
that well for you
waiting for you to decide what I mean
by the verb "draw"

I sit like a vessel
in earth
and ache when you seem not to understand

that the water which I hold
is made from the tears
which I cry
on my walls
for you.

# Art and Creation

Every artist knows some small aspect of the creator
The potter knows how God shaped the clay
A painter knows how the colors blend
A writer knows how the characters
take on a life of their own
and go ways the creator never intended.

# the material

plunge toward the most strenuous internal
simplify the material external
wait sitting still
for the wave to pass
while working on the subtle adjustments
to tuning.

# Last Day at Convocation

I woke and went to meditate
and then came back to bed

When I awoke again
a chant was running in my head
A sweet peace,
a nice way to end my retreat

I dance away
on happy feet
The Master's grace,
like an aura around me
My Guru's will
like steel within me
His linage protects
and directs me.

# Departing

As you prepare to exit
the manifest of these energies;
bear in mind, with each step
you are crossing the cosmos,
and entering another dimension.
Go gently,
aware of these voyages,
open to varying realities you
will encounter, in this, the outside
world.
Bear too, in mind,
the contented joy which enfolds you,
and for the sake of God
(and ours)
*be happy!*

# About the Author

Richard Gartee is a poet with over three hundred published poems. He is also an award-winning novelist who authored eight novels, seven college textbooks, and four nonfiction books.

A complete list of his available titles, up-coming events, and forthcoming books is available at www.gartee.com where you can find links to purchase his books, and sign up to receive updates on his newest publications as they become available.

# Canyon Falls

## Collected Poems Volume 4

in paperback and e-book

ISBN: 978-0-9895104-7-9

*Canyon Falls* is a collection of poems about love and relationships using the imagery of two distinct metaphors. It is about the moment we know we are about to fall in love, when the breath stops, but the heart races. The future appears beautiful, like the view from a canyon's rim. Sometimes we peek over the precipice and step back. Sometimes we jump in feet first anyway seeking that powerful energy of love flowing like a waterfall at the canyon's heart.

# Arbor Encore

## Collected Poems Volume 5

in paperback and e-book

ISBN: 978-1-7363957-5-2

Arbor Encore is a collection of 47 poems by Richard Gartee, which had their first publication in the renowned international poetry journal, Ann Arbor Review. Written and published over the course of five decades, during which the author became a regular Ann Arbor Review contributor.

# Skating on Skim Ice

in paperback and e-book

ISBN 978-0-9906768-2-9

Like a time traveler journeying ninety-three years from the past, Dick Gartee's life from the Roaring Twenties through the age of smart phones puts America's significant transformative decades in context.

# THE HIPPODROME THEATRE FIRST 50 YEARS

in case-laminate hardcover

ISBN 978-1-7363957-3-8

How a daring band of thespians founded a theatre that saved a dying downtown business district, became a city's cultural icon, and centerpiece of its artistic community. Includes the story of each play, cast members of most, and recollections and anecdotes from Hippodrome founders, actors, directors, and production staff illustrated with 420 photos.

Made in the USA
Monee, IL
07 July 2026